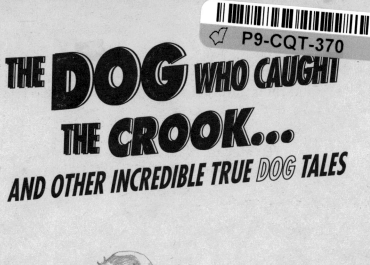

THE DOG WHO CAUGHT THE CROOK...
AND OTHER INCREDIBLE TRUE DOG TALES

by Allan Zullo and Mara Bovsun

SCHOLASTIC INC.

New York Toronto London Auckland Sydney
Mexico City New Delhi Hong Kong Buenos Aires

To Chad and Danny Manausa,
and their faithful four-legged pal, Jessie.
— A.Z.

To Megan, Maggie, and Lisa,
my three incredible dog tales.
— M.B.

We wish to thank the dog owners who
shared their interesting stories with us.

We also would like to thank Petfinder.com and the
Burlington County (New Jersey) Animal Alliance.

ISBN 0-439-66829-8

12 11 10 9 8 7 6 5 4 3 2   4 5 6 7 8 9/0

Printed in the U.S.A.   40
First printing, September 2004

Contents

Every Dog Has His Day

Dogs are brave, smart, loyal, and goofy. They are eager to play and eager to please. They ask for nothing more than a pat on the head and food in their bowl.

This book is a celebration of incredible canines — a fancy word for dogs — whose antics and adventures will astound and amuse you. For example, Yellow Dog the mutt made an official appearance in a professional baseball game. . . . Bruno the Great Dane caused a plate-smashing, glass-shattering panic in an elegant hotel. . . . Henry the retriever ran right off a 140-foot cliff and lived to chase birds again. . . . Budweiser the Saint Bernard twice ran into a burning house to rescue children. . . . Blue the Australian blue heeler fought off a huge alligator to save the life of his mistress. . . . And Punch the Labrador retriever saved a fellow hunting dog from drowning.

Whether they are strays, purebreds, or mutts, one thing is certain: Dogs are simply amazing!

Making Waves

Dogs have been known to steal all kinds of things —
birthday cakes, homework, a Thanksgiving turkey, shoes,
underwear, even a car or two. But that's nothing
compared to what Spankie the English bulldog did. She
swiped a WaveRunner, which is like a Jet Ski with seats.

Spankie had learned all by herself to ride the Wave-
Runner in 1998. She had been watching her owners,
Chuck and Kathie Webber of Ocala, Florida, zip along
the Crystal River in their watercraft. One day Kathie
was about to take a ride, when she heard Spankie howl-

3

ing from inside their houseboat. The minute Kathie opened the door, the dog shot down the pier and leaped onto the WaveRunner. She planted her rear end on the front seat and put her paws on the handlebars, like she had been born to ride.

Kathie then got on the seat behind her pet, started the machine, and the two rode the waves. From then on, Kathie never went out on the WaveRunner without her four-legged mate, who soon sported a pair of pink sunglasses and a pink doggy life jacket.

Spankie became an instant celebrity in the area. Boaters took pictures of the funny little dog in sunglasses zipping along on the WaveRunner, her tongue flapping in the wind, her head low. Sometimes her watercraft would bump into a boat, but most people didn't mind because Spankie always made everyone laugh.

Spankie loved to go fast. She learned that if she pressed down on Kathie's hand — which rested on the on/off button and the speed control — she could make the machine go faster. She'd also help Kathie steer by leaning in the direction of the turn.

Once, while they were zooming down the river, they

were stopped by the Marine Patrol. "Hey, lady," the officer said to Kathie. "Do you know you were speeding?"

"It wasn't me. It was her!" Kathie replied, pointing to her panting pal in the pink sunglasses.

When Spankie demonstrated her WaveRunner skills, the officer laughed and let Kathie off with a warning.

But that didn't stop Spankie from getting into more trouble. One time, while the dog was sitting on the WaveRunner, Kathie was in the water cleaning out some weeds that were clogging the motor.

All of a sudden, off roared Spankie, all alone on the WaveRunner. "Spankie, come back!" Kathie yelled. But it was no use. The little bulldog was crouching low on the handlebars, whizzing down the river.

Kathie scanned the river and was horrified to see a big yacht right in the bulldog's path. While Spankie knew how to balance on the seat and make the WaveRunner go fast, she didn't know how to turn by herself. Luckily, she heard her mistress's shouts and turned her head to the left to look back. That turned the WaveRunner just enough so that when her watercraft hit the wake from the passing yacht, it turned completely around.

Now it headed straight for Kathie, who was still in the water. As the WaveRunner came by, Kathie jumped up and grabbed the rubber cord that was attached to the start button and turned the machine off.

"Spankie, you are a bad girl," Kathie yelled as she climbed aboard. Although the bulldog continued to ride the WaveRunner for the rest of her life, Spankie never again did it solo.

White House Terror

No dog in the White House was a worse rascal than Pete.

The mischievous bull terrier was owned by Teddy Roosevelt, who, during his two terms in office (1901–1909), had more pets than most any other president.

The Executive Mansion burst at the seams with dogs, cats, squirrels, raccoons, rabbits, guinea pigs, a badger, a bear, a rat, a parrot, and a snake. But none caused more trouble than Pete.

The dog snapped at government officials and chased newspaper reporters. He ran after visitors' cars, following them for such long distances that he would get lost. Police would have to search the city until they found him and returned him to the president.

At an important White House dinner in 1907, Pete

created an international incident. For no reason at all, he ripped the pants of the French ambassador.

The dog roamed the White House grounds and made it his life's ambition to chase people. Visitors without official escorts had to be fast runners if they hoped to make it safely across the White House lawn without having teeth marks on their legs. Some weren't fast enough, including members of the president's own staff.

One morning, Pete went after John Thomas, an official from the Department of the Navy. Thomas was walking in front of the White House when he spotted the dog racing toward him. Thomas ran as fast as he could, hoping to reach the safety of the nearest tree. Just as Thomas started climbing the tree, Pete leaped up and clamped onto the man's right leg — and wouldn't let go. White House police arrived and tried to yank the dog off him, but Pete held on for several minutes before they pried him away. Thomas limped back to his office, missing most of the right leg of his pants.

Said Thomas, who was treated for bite wounds by a Navy doctor, "I have been told that it is a distinction [honor] to be bitten by the president's dog, but I would have preferred not to."

Just two days later, Pete got a taste of his own medicine. A stray white bull terrier slipped through the White House gate and attacked Pete. When police stopped the fight with a bucket of water, Pete ran back to the White House, yelping all the way with his tail tucked between his legs.

Wrong Time for Playtime

Because a big dog was lonely and wanted to find a human to play with, the kitchen staff of a world-class hotel fled in food-flying, plate-smashing panic.

The dog, a Great Dane named Bruno, belonged to a guest at New York City's expensive Waldorf-Astoria Hotel in 1905. Because dogs weren't allowed in the rooms, Bruno was put in the baggage room for the evening. A bellhop fed the friendly dog, secured him with a long rope, and closed the door.

Although there were other dogs in the room, Bruno was used to being with his master and his master's family and friends. He wanted to be around people so much that he was determined to escape. He chewed on his rope until it broke. Then he tried opening the door by pushing on it with his front paws, but it wouldn't budge.

Upset that he couldn't get out, Bruno began howling louder and louder until he was heard throughout the hotel. After half an hour, assistant manager A. W. Little went to the baggage room to calm the dog. But when Little opened the door, Bruno bounded out and romped down the hall.

The playful Great Dane sprang joyfully at a bellhop and knocked him down. When the bellhop tried to get up, Bruno jumped on him and flattened him again. Then the dog ran off in search of someone to play with.

Bruno entered the dish pantry where several women were putting away the hotel's fine china. The woman who was nearest the door didn't notice that the dog had entered the room. When he playfully rubbed against her, she screamed in terror, "It's a bear!" Then she dropped an armful of plates. In their rush to get away from the "bear," the other women in the room scattered as cups, saucers, and bowls crashed to the floor.

Somewhat discouraged by their reaction, Bruno dashed out of the room and into the kitchen. The cooks, chefs, and assistants weren't used to seeing a dog — especially a giant one — in the kitchen. They shouted warnings in their native tongues of French, German, and Italian. As food went flying from dropped pots and pans, they scrambled out of the room.

Meanwhile, the dessert chef, who was hard of hearing, was busy filling a fancy pastry shell with a special cream and didn't pay any attention to the chaos around him. When Bruno came up to him and gave him a friendly nuzzle, the chef jerked up in total shock. He dropped his prized dessert, which the dog was only too willing to gobble up.

While Bruno was licking the last of the sweet cream off the floor, two hotel workers collared the dog and dragged him back to the baggage room. This time, they tied him with a chain and kept a bellhop in the room to keep him company — and to keep him quiet. As for Bruno's owner, he was billed for all the broken china and ruined food that his playful dog had caused.

Conan's Candy Caper

Conan the pit bull terrier had a big sweet tooth — one that got him into trouble with the law.

One morning in 2003, shortly before dawn, Conan woke up with a terrible craving for a sugary treat. No one was awake, so he sneaked out of his owner's house in Oslo, Norway, shortly before dawn. The seven-year-old dog then headed straight for the only place that was open, the Statoil gas station, which also was a small convenience store.

Security cameras caught him walking through the automatic door, sniffing the candy shelves, and poking his nose into the containers of sweets. He snubbed all of these treats in search of his personal favorite — chocolate-covered rice crisp. As soon as he found it, he ripped open the container and gobbled the goodies. When he was finished, he let out an enormous burp.

Elisabeth Roel, who was working the night shift at the station, tried to chase Conan out, but the dog growled at her for interrupting his chocolate raid.

The clerk wouldn't have been so worried if she had recognized Conan. But because he had escaped without his collar and tags, she wasn't sure whether or not he was a mean, stray dog. Not wanting to take chances, she called a security guard, who nabbed the dog and put him behind bars for the night.

This wasn't the first time Conan had stolen treats from a store, admitted his embarrassed owner, Liss-Hege Jeremiassen. "He is incredibly fond of food in general and sweets in particular," she said. "He has run off a few times before, and he always heads for food stores."

Bill the Bandit

After roaming around the neighborhood, Bill the bull terrier often brought some sort of gift home to his owner. Unfortunately, the presents he so proudly gave his mistress were never anything that she wanted. Besides, they were stolen.

Having a thief for a dog was bad enough. But it was especially troubling for Bill's owner, Loretta Cody, because she was the daughter of a lieutenant in the New Rochelle (New York) Police Department.

Bill would bring home things such as old shoes that people had left out on their doorsteps, cans from rubbish heaps, and underwear that had been drying on clotheslines. Bill also showed up with gifts of food. One time he brought Loretta a bag of rolls that he had swiped from someone's grocery sack. Another time he came home splattered with milk, having tried to carry a full bottle of milk.

But in 1916, it looked like the canine bandit had crossed the line from being a petty thief to a major criminal. He dragged home a lady's handbag. When Loretta went through the purse, she found a large sum of money inside. She also found an ID belonging to Mrs. Stephen W. Huntington, wife of the vice president of the city council of New Rochelle. They were very important people in town.

Embarrassed beyond belief, Loretta went to Mrs. Huntington's house and returned the purse while offering apologies for her shameful dog. But Mrs. Huntington laughed and explained that what Bill had done was really a good thing. He hadn't stolen the purse, she said. He had *found* it.

Mrs. Huntington explained that she had placed her purse on top of her car and then forgot about it and drove off. It had fallen somewhere in the street, and she thought she had lost it for good. But Bill found the purse and brought it home — with nothing missing inside.

Bill, the little rascal, was then given a new collar as a reward for his honesty.

Touching All the Bases

A little yellow mutt made history by officially appearing in a professional baseball game.

The pooch was a stray who was adopted by Roberto Ortiz, a member of the minor-league team the Charlotte Hornets. Ortiz named him Yellow Dog.

Every day the mutt tagged along as Ortiz walked to a nearby restaurant for dinner. The dog waited outside until Ortiz finished his meal and fed him the leftovers. At night, Ortiz bunked in a little apartment beneath the left-field bleachers while Yellow Dog slept by the door.

When the team worked out, the mutt romped alongside Ortiz. Each day when Ortiz completed batting practice, he raced around the bases and Yellow Dog — his ears flopping in the wind — ran along with him. Ortiz taught the mutt not only to touch the bases but also to slide, by rolling over at full speed. The canine slide cracked up everyone who saw it. However, team officials told Ortiz that the dog had to be locked up in his apartment during games.

Before a 1941 game against Norfolk, Ortiz accidentally left the apartment door open. So after a nap, the mutt ambled along the foul line toward the dugout during the game. It was the bottom of the ninth inning and Charlotte was down by a run. After the first batter walked, Ortiz socked the ball off the center-field wall and was steaming around first base when a yellow blur joined him. It was Yellow Dog scampering at his master's heels. Down to second they went, but they didn't stop there.

Ortiz slid into third . . . and so did Yellow Dog. The fans and umpire stared in disbelief as Yellow Dog curled up into a rolling slide, arriving just behind Ortiz. The umpire peered into the cloud of dust and gave the "safe" sign twice, first for Ortiz and then for the pooch. The fans roared with laughter. Ortiz got up, dusted himself off, and handed Yellow Dog to the team trainer.

The next day the *Charlotte News* ran the official box score of the game. In the space reserved for pinch runners, it read: "Yellow Dog ran with Ortiz in the ninth."

Seal of Approval

Seal was a cross-eyed black-and-white mongrel who became the University of Virginia's mascot in the late 1940s. Only one thing inspired him at football games: During halftime, he would pee on the goalposts of the opposing team.

His sleek coat of fur earned him the name Seal, and he later became known as the "Great Seal of Virginia." The beloved mascot was allowed in the university's lecture halls and nearly everywhere else around town. Local restaurants had signs reading: "No Dogs Allowed Except Seal." He was fed by different fraternities as well as by the staff at the university's cafeteria.

His greatest feat came at Franklin Field in Philadelphia when Virginia played the University of Pennsylvania in 1949.

Wearing a blue blanket with a large orange "V," Seal

headed for the Penn goalposts seconds before the half-time gun sounded. He was planning to pee on them. But the Penn cheerleaders formed a line, blocking the dog's path. Seal thought about this problem for a moment. Then he ran straight for the cheerleaders' empty bench and peed on it. The Virginia fans went wild, and the team went on to win its seventh straight game, 26–14.

Seal was about ten years old and suffering from stomach problems when he was put to sleep in 1953. About 1,500 people attended his funeral. An antique black hearse carried his flower-draped casket as drums beat out a slow death march. Behind the hearse walked students, townspeople, and school officials. Seal was laid to rest at the University Cemetery alongside the school's only other canine mascot, Beta, who lived on campus in the 1930s.

Ice Capade

Rocky the Labrador retriever tried to ice-fish once, but his way was simply too outrageous.

Each winter when a Minnesota lake called Mille Lac freezes over, about 2,500 ice-fishermen put up their shacks on the frozen surface. Inside their shacks, fishermen cut holes in the ice and fish for walleye, crappie, and pike.

On a bone-chilling day in 1967, Frank Linquist of Minneapolis brought along his pet dog Rocky as he waited patiently inside his shack for a fish to take his bait. The Lab, on his first ice-fishing trip, kept staring at the hole. Suddenly, a large pike swam right across the hole just below the water's surface. Rocky leaped to his feet and barked excitedly.

Then the dog jumped headfirst into the hole after the fish! The pike darted away, but Rocky swam after it, going deeper and deeper under the thick gray sheet of ice. By the time the Labrador realized he could never catch the fast-moving fish, he was hopelessly lost and trapped under the ice.

The dog frantically paddled back and forth, desperately searching for the hole that he had dived from. But he was running out of time. Just when it seemed he would drown, he saw a shaft of light beaming down from a hole in the ice. Rocky swam to it, not knowing the hole was in another shack thirty feet away from his master's.

The dog's head popped out of the water, shocking the fisherman who, in a lifetime of fishing, had never landed a stranger catch.

Dog-tired, Rocky finally scrambled out of the hole. Shivering from the frigid water, he furiously shook his body, showering the still-stunned fisherman from head to toe. Minutes later, the diving dog and his worried master were reunited.

As for the surprised fisherman, he had a whopper of a story to tell his friends about his latest catch: "Well, fellas, it was four feet long, had big ears, was covered with fur. . . ."

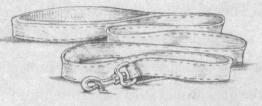

Odd Couple

For a beagle, Blackie was sort of a quack. That's because his best friend was a duck named — what else? — Mr. Duck.

The two were always together on the small farm of John Vrabely Sr. in Economy, Pennsylvania. It was a strange relationship, considering the fact that most beagles are known to hunt ducks.

But Blackie was a gentle soul who seemed to like all the animals on the farm. So in 1998, when Blackie was nine years old, he didn't cause any trouble when the farmer was given six ducks. Unfortunately, over the next two years, all the ducks died except Mr. Duck.

Without his own kind to play with, the lonely Mr. Duck struck up a friendship with Blackie. The beagle was more than happy to be the pal and guardian of his new feathered buddy. They played in a nearby creek, shared the same food, and cuddled up with each other at night. Mr. Duck learned to stick close to Blackie for protection whenever the duck would steal food from the farm cats.

The dog and duck never wandered off the property, except on one weekend in 2002, when they failed to return home after being gone all day. Gerard Vrabely, who had inherited the farm following his father's death, began searching for the pair without success.

Later that night, a quarter mile away, teenager Jason Kratochvil and his friends were out on the front porch of his home when they heard a quacking noise. That's when Blackie and Mr. Duck strolled into the yard.

Believing the animals were someone's pets and fearing for their safety on the dark streets at eleven P.M., Jason's mother, Juanita, decided the strange pair could stay. She herded the animals into her laundry room and fed them while her daughter, Nicole, called the police. The cops thought it was a prank. Come on, a dog and a duck? No one had reported them missing. After some convincing, the police took Nicole's name and number.

Meanwhile, Mr. Duck, apparently bored with a steady diet of crackers, stuck his beak into Blackie's dish and ate some of his dog food. That night the duck slept with his head buried in the beagle's pepper-colored fur. "It's just so comical," Juanita told her family. "There really is a gentleness between them. They're a team."

The next day, Juanita phoned the *Beaver County Times*, the local newspaper, which published a story and photo about the dog and duck. Vrabely saw the article and immediately called Juanita.

"I never expected them to be here," Vrabely told her when he showed up to get the animals. Grinning, he added, "These are my bad kids. They're grounded."

His Brother's Keeper

Although Ludwig the miniature poodle was born blind, he had an active, full life because he had his own guide dog — his brother Gunther.

Richard and Pat Schoppmeyer of Bohemia, New York, went to a breeder in 1971 and bought Gunther, who was the ugly runt of a litter of eight. Even so, the couple fell in love with him.

After they brought Gunther home, the puppy cried for four straight days. Meanwhile, the Schoppmeyers learned that the last remaining puppy from the litter also had been crying nonstop, so they bought him, too, and named him Ludwig.

They soon noticed that Ludwig followed Gunther everywhere and seemed very dependent on him. The couple had Ludwig's eyes tested and learned he was blind. But it was no big deal to Ludwig because his brother had become his personal escort. Guided by Gunther, Ludwig learned his way around the Schoppmeyers' house and their one-acre yard.

The blind dog could follow a ball by the sound of the bounce. However, whenever he lost contact with Gunther while they were playing, he would just sit down and wait until Gunther came over and nudged him. Ludwig loved to climb on anything he could, but he was always afraid to get down. So Gunther would have to come over and give him a gentle poke. Then Ludwig would jump down without fear.

The two dogs romped in the back around trees and bushes and barreled up and down the stairs, with Ludwig always close to his seeing-eye brother.

Postal Pooches

Two neighborhood dogs helped deliver the mail for twelve years through rain and shine.

Butch, a beagle, and Jeff, a collie–German shepherd mix, would wait at the same corner in New Rochelle, New York, for mailman William Riley to show up. Riley would greet them cheerily, let them carry mail in their mouths, and talk to them as they trotted at his side over his two-mile postal route.

The neighbors enjoyed seeing the postal pooches. Housewives would save bones to hand to the mailman, who carried them to the end of his route before giving Butch and Jeff their daily treats.

"It's the darndest thing the way they help Mr. Riley," said the dogs' owner, Mrs. Raymond Comyns. "Those dogs are so smart that they never missed a weekday, but they always knew not to go out to meet him on his days off." They followed the same daily routine from 1938 to 1950.

But then one day, a different mailman showed up. He loved animals and warmly greeted the surprised dogs. He gently put mail in their mouths, but their tails didn't wag and their feet didn't move. He tried to sweet-talk them into joining him, but they still refused. He took the letters out of their mouths and went on his route without them.

The next day, as a chilly rain fell, Butch and Jeff again waited for Mr. Riley to show up so they could help him deliver the mail, just as they had done for a dozen years. But it was not to be. Mr. Riley, their postal pal, had died unexpectedly. Without Mr. Riley, the dogs never delivered another letter again.

The Dog Who Wouldn't Stay Behind

The loyalty of some dogs is so strong that nothing can keep them apart from their masters, not even war.

Sergeant François Jacquimin of the French army was stationed in the African country of Algeria, where he adopted a springer spaniel he named Feu-de-l'Air (French for "Fire of the Air"). The dog adored his master. But when World War I began in 1914, the sergeant said good-bye to his beloved dog and prepared to ship off to fight in France.

As the transport ship moved away from the pier, the sergeant waved a tearful farewell to his dog back on the dock. But Feu-de-l'Air wasn't about to watch his master sail away without him. The dog jumped into the water and started swimming toward the boat. Touched by his devotion, the soldiers ordered the ship to stop. Then

Sergeant Jacquimin scrambled down a ladder and tied a rope around his dog. Amid cheers and applause, the spaniel was hoisted aboard.

After arriving in France, the sergeant's regiment got on a train bound for the battlefield in Belgium to fight the German army. Once again, Sergeant Jacquimin had to say good-bye to his dog. And once again, the dog ignored orders to stay. While the soldiers boarded the train, the dog sneaked into one of the supply boxcars and hid behind some crates. When the train reached its final destination in Belgium, Feu-de-l'Air astonished the entire regiment when he suddenly appeared at the feet of Sergeant Jacquimin. Admiring the loyalty of this remarkable canine, the commanding officer allowed the dog to unofficially enlist and join his master in battle.

Months later, during a heavy attack by German artillery, a shell exploded in the trench where the sergeant and his men had been holed up. Twelve soldiers were killed. A dozen more were seriously wounded, including Sergeant Jacquimin. He was buried under splintered wooden beams, rocks, and dirt when the sides of the trench collapsed. His legs and hands were badly injured, and shrapnel (pieces of the artillery shell) had pierced his back.

Despite his wounds, the sergeant was conscious but unable to move. He could barely breathe and knew he had only a few minutes left before he would suffocate under all the debris. Just before he passed out, he thought he heard his dog barking.

Meanwhile, moments after the blast, Feu-de-l'Air, who was not hurt, raced over to the spot where his master was buried and began digging and barking furiously. Seeing medics nearby, the dog raced over to one of them, seized the medic's shirt in his teeth, and led him to the mound. Then the dog and the medic dug through the rubble until they reached the sergeant. He was pulled out alive and rushed to a field hospital, accompanied by his faithful canine companion.

But when Sergeant Jacquimin was later transferred to a hospital near Paris, officers wouldn't let the dog go with him. Although they treated the dog well, Feu-de-l'Air refused to eat because he missed his master so much. Two days later, the officers had a change of heart and shipped the dog to the hospital, where he was washed, combed, and disinfected. He stayed by the bed of the sergeant until the soldier was well enough to go home.

Later, Sergeant Jacquimin was awarded the French Military Medal of Honor. By his side was Feu-de-l'Air — the loyal dog who refused to be left behind.

Well Done

A German shepherd pup saved the life of her best friend — a Labrador retriever.

Sierra, a seven-month-old puppy, and Bowdie, a two-year-old black Lab, ate together, played together, and slept together at the home of their owner, Stephanie Whetsell of Ventura, California.

One day in 1996, the dogs slipped out of the backyard while Stephanie was at work. They spent the morning frolicking in the neighborhood, but the fun stopped when the ninety-pound Lab fell thirty feet down a dark, cramped, abandoned well that had been covered with wood planks.

Hearing her pal howling, Sierra frantically dug trenches around the hole in a desperate attempt to free Bowdie. Seeing that her efforts were useless, Sierra raced to the nearest house for help. Jayne Cooper was getting ready for a business meeting when she looked up and saw a whimpering puppy on its hind legs peering through her kitchen window.

After Jayne stepped outside, the dog led her to the abandoned well about thirty yards away. She saw Bowdie — shivering and mud-caked — trapped in the bottom. It was so cramped that the Lab's snout and tail were touching the walls. Jayne stuck a ladder down the well, but the dog was too frightened to climb out, so she phoned 911. When firefighters arrived, Sierra nervously paced back and forth until an animal control officer moved her away. The puppy whined every time she heard Bowdie's frantic bark.

But as firefighters prepared to lower a rescuer into the well, Bowdie stopped barking because he was running out of air in the clammy hole. Fresh air was immediately pumped into the well, and Bowdie began barking again. Minutes later, the rescuer made his way down to the scared, wet dog.

The rescuer put a harness and muzzle on Bowdie, and the two were brought to the surface. Tail wagging, Bowdie raced over to Sierra and rubbed noses with the puppy who had saved his life — his best friend.

A Friend in Need

During a hunting trip, a Labrador retriever named
Punch did more than retrieve birds. He retrieved his good
buddy — a drowning dog.

Punch and his master, W. A. Lake, went pheasant hunting with Malcolm Jones and his golden retriever, Jill,
near Norfolk, England, in the winter of 1952. The hunters
were having a good day shooting pheasant out of the sky,
and the dogs were having fun retrieving the fallen birds.

Late in the afternoon, Jones shot a bird that fell into a
nearby river. Jill, as she had been doing all day, galloped
after the latest downed pheasant and plunged into the
chilly water. But as she neared the bird, Jill suffered a
severe cramp. She stopped swimming and began to sink.

Seeing that his friend was in trouble, Punch dashed into
the frigid river and swam out to the drowning dog. With
his teeth, Punch grabbed Jill by the back of the neck and

then towed her to the bank where Jones pulled her out. Jill was semiconscious but after getting a thorough massage from her master, she was fully revived.

Punch stayed by her side until he knew she would be all right. Then he jumped back into the river and retrieved the pheasant that Jill's master had shot down.

Tough but Tender

Blackie, a German shepherd who was trained to be a snarling guard dog, had a soft spot for his pal Loco the cat. So when Loco was killed shortly after giving birth to a litter, the dog stepped in to care for her seven orphaned kittens.

Blackie was a watchdog at the Mister Lucky Dog Training School in Brooklyn, New York, and often demonstrated how to attack intruders. Despite his fierce reputation, the dog acted like a pussycat around his feline friend, Loco, the school's mascot. He was always gentle with her and made sure no one threatened her.

When Loco gave birth to her litter in 1966, Blackie stood guard over the newborns. He wouldn't let anyone into the room.

But then tragedy struck. Leaving her kittens in her bed, Loco went out for a walk and was hit by a car and killed.

When Loco failed to return, Blackie came to the aid of the defenseless kitties. While owner Les Spiewack nursed them with a bottle, the dog took on some of the cat's responsibilities. If any of the kittens wandered off, he would find it and gently carry it in his teeth back to its bed.

"One of the kittens was so small that we thought it would die," Les recalled. "Blackie removed it from the rest of the litter and massaged it in his jaws until it was ready to hold its own in the battle with the others for the milk.

"Blackie was a very tough dog, but with a tender heart."

Bozo's Buddies

No one knew where Bozo came from. The reddish-brown mongrel — a mixture of chow, collie, and German shepherd — showed up one day in the Astoria neighborhood of Queens, New York, and instantly became a friend of all the kids.

Owned by none but beloved by all, Bozo would spend the night at one child's house and then have a sleepover with another kid on the following night. Almost every day he would accept food from a different family. No matter where or when he showed up, he was always welcome.

But the fact that he was officially a stray dog without a license nearly cost him his freedom — and almost his life. Fortunately, the kids who adored him came to his rescue.

In 1941, word spread throughout the neighborhood that someone had called the police, demanding that they catch the unlicensed dog and take him away. When the kids couldn't find Bozo so they could hide him, they staged a massive demonstration.

That afternoon, two patrolmen drove up and were met by fifty children who pleaded, "Please don't take our Bozo!" Several kids carried hand-lettered signs that read: "Let Us Keep Bozo" and "Don't Take Our Pal Bozo." Even family dogs took part. A German shepherd named Toni carried a sign around her neck that read "I Want My Boyfriend Bozo" while Boots the dachshund's sign read "Let Me Keep My Pal Bozo."

Impressed by the support and love for the missing mongrel, the policemen promised not to take Bozo away on the condition that the kids follow the law and get a license, leash, and muzzle for him.

The kids were thrilled that Bozo would be allowed to stay in the neighborhood. They quickly collected $2.80 in pennies, nickels, and dimes to pay for everything the dog needed to be legal.

So where was Bozo during all the fuss? After learning that authorities were looking for the dog, one of the neighborhood kids had hidden him in the cellar of his home until it was safe to come out.

The Pooch and the Pip-squeak

A Great Dane and a pet mouse struck up an unusual friendship — one that was tested by a fainting woman, a car crash, and a chase down a busy street.

When guests came over to his house, wealthy New York businessman John J. Dooley liked to show off his pet mouse, which wore a green ribbon around its neck. He enjoyed guests' faces when they watched the little rodent play with his Great Dane, Molineux. It was quite a sight to see the tiny mouse crawl around and under the big dog.

Dooley showed off his mouse to friends at a picnic he was hosting in 1903. But later, to the man's sorrow, the mouse disappeared, and no one could find it. The next day, Molineux sulked around the house and seemed sad not to have his little buddy around, so Dooley took the dog to his office in Manhattan.

In a garage next to the office, Molineux kept sniffing around a car owned by John McCafferty, who had attended Dooley's picnic. Later that day, McCafferty decided to take a friend of his, Miss Fran Finnerty, for a ride in his car. As they drove out of the garage, Molineux dashed after the car. McCafferty shouted at the dog to go back but Molineux kept chasing it for several blocks.

Suddenly, Miss Finnerty screamed in terror and fainted. When McCafferty turned to see what had happened to her, he lost control of the car. It veered off the street, went onto a sidewalk, and crashed into a tree. McCafferty, who wasn't injured, ran to the other side of the car to check on Miss Finnerty. When he opened the door, a mouse jumped out. The woman quickly recovered and shouted, "Oh! Oh! It was a mouse! He ran up my leg!"

"It's gone," McCafferty said. "There is nothing to fear." Just then he looked down the road and saw Molineux chasing the mouse. When the dog caught it, McCafferty thought that was the end of the mouse. But Molineux was very gentle with it and brought it back in his mouth to McCafferty. Only then did the man see that the mouse had a green ribbon. "Why, it's Mr. Dooley's mouse!" he declared. The dog had not hurt it a bit.

When the mouse and the dog were returned to Dooley, he gave McCafferty $200 and Miss Finnerty $100 as a reward. As for Molineux, he was just as happy as his master to have their pet mouse back.

Comeback Canine

When Maxie was adopted out by animal shelter owner Julie Brown, Julie thought she would never again see the white German shepherd. After all, the dog had been taken by a family who lived 150 miles away.

But Maxie never forgot the love she had received from Julie. Incredibly, three years later, the dog returned on her own to the surprised woman — even though Julie by then had closed down the shelter and moved.

In 1998, Julie operated the town's animal shelter out of her home in Lubec, Maine. One of the dogs she took in was an abandoned German shepherd female pup who had a scar over her eye. The dog, who Julie named Maxie, stayed at the shelter for a year and a half.

In 2000, a couple from Palermo, Maine, stopped by the shelter and asked to adopt Maxie. They had a black German shepherd, and they said they wanted a white one to keep him company. Figuring the dog was going to a good home, Julie reluctantly let Maxie go.

But then in the fall of 2003, Julie heard about a white German shepherd hanging around the Whiting Bay area, about ten miles from where her former shelter was located.

Soon the dog was sniffing behind the shop where Julie now worked in the town of Whiting. Julie went outside hoping to get near the dog. She gave her some food and told her, "Oh, I used to have a dog that looks just like you." The dog didn't run off but she wouldn't let Julie get too close to her.

Julie returned to work two days later and again saw the dog. When she placed a dish of dog food beside her and sat down, the German shepherd came up and started licking her face. Julie then saw the scar over the dog's eye. "Maxie! It's you!" she shouted with glee. She hugged Maxie, who looked very thin but healthy.

More than 150 miles separates Whiting and Palermo. No one knows how the dog found her. But Julie and Maxie are sure glad she did.

NEVER-SAY-DIE DOGS
WHO CHEATED DEATH

Off the Hook

When Lacy the puppy got her neck tangled in a phone cord and was choking to death, she saved her own life — by dialing for help.

One day in 1999, the eight-week-old shepherd-husky mix was alone at the home of her owners, Ray and Cathy Regimbald of North Bay, Ontario, Canada. Lacy was playing with the phone when the cord somehow wrapped around her neck and she couldn't breathe.

While struggling to free herself, the choking puppy knocked the receiver off the hook and, by sheer luck, stepped on the "O" key on the phone. That connected her to an operator. Hearing the howls and whimpers of a dog in distress, the operator forwarded the call to a 911 dispatcher who traced the call and got an address for the police.

Officer Dan Robertson rushed to the house. As soon as he got out of the car, he could hear Lacy yelping inside. Seeing that the house was locked and time was running out for the dying dog, Robertson squeezed through an unlocked kitchen window.

The officer raced into the living room and found Lacy hopelessly tangled in the phone cord. It was wrapped around her neck like a noose. He quickly disconnected the phone and untied the cord that had been wound tightly around her. Luckily, the dog was not hurt. She immediately began running around the house because she was so happy to be free. She even licked the officer's face.

The puppy went right back to being her playful self, except for one thing: She never again went near the telephone.

On the Cutting Edge

Jake the puppy bit off more than he could chew . . . and it nearly cost him his life.

The twelve-week-old Staffordshire bull terrier accidentally swallowed a kitchen knife that was nearly the entire length of his body!

In 2003, the pup's owners, John Mallett and Brian Sumner of Liverpool, England, noticed that something was wrong with Jake. He had a badly swollen tummy and couldn't curl up. He kept trying to keep his body in a straight line.

The owners rushed Jake to the People's Dispensary for Sick Animals. X rays revealed why the puppy was so sick. A seven-inch kitchen knife was in his body, with the plastic handle at the base of his stomach and the blunted metal point at the top of his throat. The vet operated on the puppy immediately and within a few days, Jake was back to his old playful self.

How Jake managed to swallow a knife — let alone one that big — remains a mystery. "Dogs are always swallowing strange things, from kebab sticks to corn on the cobs to tape cassettes," said the clinic's senior veterinarian, Christina Symonds. "But this was particularly unusual because it was such a large knife in a small puppy. It really did run the length of his body." Luckily, Jake had swallowed the plastic handle of the knife first or else he could have been in much more serious trouble, she added.

Dog Paddle

Todd the Labrador retriever loved to go sailing on his master's yacht. But one day in 2002, the two-year-old dog fell overboard and disappeared off an island known as the Isle of Wight near the coast of England.

His owner, Peter Loizou, spent four frantic hours searching the choppy seas for his pet, but finally gave up hope of ever seeing him again.

However, Peter hadn't counted on Todd's determination to survive.

When the Lab plunged into the water, he didn't head for the Isle of Wight, which was only a mile away from the boat. Instead, he swam for the English shore across the busy shipping lane in a waterway known as the Solent. Paddling mightily against offshore winds that were pushing him in the opposite direction, Todd kept swimming toward the coast of England — because that was where his home was.

Even when he was close to the shoreline, he didn't head for dry land. He kept swimming, this time up the River Beaulieu, somehow knowing that it would be a more direct route to his home. Ten miles and six hours of paddling later, the exhausted Lab climbed up the riverbank at the village of Beaulieu, just eight miles from his home in Windsor, Hampshire, southwest of London.

But he was too tired to walk any farther. A sixteen-year-old boy found Todd and took him to the police, who scanned a microchip that had been implanted under the dog's skin and identified him. He was then reunited with his relieved owner, who called the dog's survival an "absolute miracle."

From then on, Todd had to wear a doggy life vest whenever he went sailing with his master.

Heading for a Fall

Henry the retriever was concentrating so hard on chasing and catching a seagull that the dog ran right off a cliff and plunged 140 feet into the ocean. Unbelievably, he lived to chase again.

The dog was walking with his owner, Louise Chavannes, near the edge of Seven Sisters cliffs in Sussex, England, in 2001. Suddenly, he ran after a low-flying seagull. When the two reached the edge of the cliff, the bird flew off . . . and so did the dog. But, unlike the bird, Henry didn't have wings. He headed straight down toward the rocky surf below.

Louise was convinced he was dead and couldn't bear the thought of his body floating in the sea. But when she got to the edge of the cliff where he had jumped off, she couldn't believe it. Henry was swimming to the shore.

Louise struggled down hundreds of steps and ran along

half a mile of beach to reach him. Fortunately, Henry had leaped so far out from the cliff top that when he fell, he missed slamming into the rocks below. Instead, he crashed directly into the ocean. His only injury was a broken leg.

Said local veterinarian Peter Stotesbury: "No one could believe he had survived a fall from that height. He is the luckiest dog we have ever come across."

Miracle Girl

Some dogs obviously don't know that only cats are supposed to have nine lives.

Take Dosha, for instance. In the span of three hours, she was struck by a car, shot in the head, stuffed into a body bag, and put in a freezer. And she lived to bark about it.

In 2003, Dosha, a ten-month-old mongrel, slipped out of the fenced-in backyard of her owner, Louetta Mallard of Clearlake, California. Minutes after her escape, Dosha was hit by a car.

As the badly injured dog lay on the side of the road, a passerby called the local police department. Officer Bob MacDonald arrived on the scene and thought the dog was a stray because she wasn't wearing a collar. To end her suffering, Officer MacDonald shot Dosha below the right eye. The dog's limp body was put into a body bag and taken to the city's animal control center, where it was put into the freezer. The center planned to incinerate (burn) the body.

Two hours later, when the center's director, Denise Johnson, opened the freezer, she was shocked to find Dosha sitting up in the bag, semiconscious and shivering — and still clinging to life.

Dosha was rushed to Clearlake Veterinary Clinic, where she was treated by Dr. Deborah Sally. The dog was suffering from hypothermia, or loss of body heat, so the first thing the vet did was put warm blankets on her. Next Dosha was taken for X rays, which showed she had a broken cheekbone from the car and a hole in her head from the bullet. The vet operated on the dog.

Dosha made a remarkable recovery and returned home ten days after her near-death experience. She became an overnight celebrity with appearances on morning talk shows and in newspaper articles throughout the world.

Said Dr. Sally, "When she first came in, we couldn't believe what she had gone through and was still with us. We called her Miracle Girl."

Go With the Floe

Scooter, an American foxhound, had gone for a walk with her master during a snowfall . . . and ended up a lonely castaway for days on an ice floe drifting out to sea.

Her unplanned adventure in 2001 began while she and her master, Jeremy Millar, were playing in the snow near Big Point, Prince Edward Island, Canada. When the two-year-old dog spotted a coyote, she gave chase and ran onto the ice. Millar tried to keep up but he eventually lost sight of her when the snowfall turned into a blinding snowstorm.

At first Millar wasn't too worried because Scooter was wearing a transmitter around her neck. But efforts to track her were unsuccessful. When the storm ended, Millar discovered that the ice where he had last seen his dog had broken off and had carried her out into the Northumberland Strait. Chances of finding her alive seemed slim.

Five days later, Rick Kehoe, a construction worker at Lismore, Nova Scotia, spotted Scooter on an ice floe. She was running back and forth on the ice, but there was no place for her to go because she was surrounded by frigid water. Kehoe knew he had to save her. Using a boat, he went out to the ice floe and coaxed her aboard.

Although she had lost weight, Scooter was in remarkably healthy condition. She was soon dining on salmon, chicken, turkey, and roast beef given to her by residents of Lismore.

The dog's incredible journey had carried her more than forty miles across the Northumberland Strait. The tides had been pushing her back and forth between Prince Edward Island and Nova Scotia for days.

The identification tag on her collar made it possible for Kehoe to contact Millar, who was soon happily reunited with his hound — a hound who no longer chased coyotes on the ice.

A "Hole" Lot of Trouble

Maggie, a five-year-old terrier, had gone off to chase a rabbit. The bunny showed up again, but Maggie didn't.

For nearly a month in 2001, the gray short-haired dog remained missing. Her owner, Errol Hilton, a farmer in New Zealand, was heartbroken. He figured that an animal had killed her.

One day Hilton was moving some cows when he heard a familiar bark coming from a nearby bush. He was surprised because it sounded just like Maggie. But then he thought it was his imagination caused by the heartache over his missing dog. The farmer stood still and held his breath. Sure enough, he heard it again. He followed the sound to a tiny rabbit hole, which was the size of a tennis ball.

Although Hilton couldn't see into the dark hole, he heard breathing coming from inside it. He quickly ran for a shovel and then started digging. He dug about two feet down, stuck his hand inside, and felt a licking tongue. It was Maggie!

After Hilton pulled her out, the dog joyously celebrated her freedom by running around in circles for several minutes before plopping down exhausted in front of her very happy owner.

Apparently, while chasing the rabbit, Maggie ended up trapped in the bunny hole and couldn't get out. She had lost nearly half her weight from her twenty-nine day underground ordeal. A dog can survive many weeks without food but must have water. Maggie managed to survive on rainwater that had dripped into the hole.

When Maggie returned home, her master let her dine on her favorite meal — scrambled eggs and rice pudding. There was no rabbit stew.

A Taste for Golf

A yellow Labrador named Hannah lived, breathed, and ate golf. And that got her in a tummy full of trouble.

The dog, owned by Loretta and Scott Sullivan of Cherry Hill, New Jersey, loved to retrieve golf balls that his owners would hit in a nearby field. "We'd go through a bag full of balls and she'd bolt after them," Loretta said. "We aren't real golfers. In fact, we were hitting balls just for her. Her whole thing was collecting them, going from one ball to the next one, getting them in her mouth, and then running back and dropping them in front of us. She loved it and got lots of exercise. This went on for two years.

"But one day in October 1997, she got sick and started vomiting. We took her to the vet and at first he thought it was a virus. But then they did an X ray, and when they finished, I could hear them laughing in the back room."

No wonder. The X rays revealed nine golf balls bunched in Hannah's stomach!

"I was in amazement," said Loretta. "They opened her stomach, pulled out the balls, and gave them to me.

"When we first started playing golf with her, I had been worried that she'd choke on the balls so I always kept count of how many I started with and finished with. But other people played golf with her — the pet-sitter, relatives, neighbors. And who was counting? We think that she put so many balls in her mouth at one time that some had slipped down her throat."

Hannah's golfing days were over for good.

Leaping Lulu

Just hours after being saved from death row, Lulu the Chihuahua faced possible death again. This time, it was from jumping out of her new owner's car, which was zooming down a busy interstate highway at seventy miles an hour.

The tiny pooch had been in an Alabama animal shelter that was planning to put her down because nobody wanted her. But Nan LaSalle of the Small Dog Rescue in Atlanta, Georgia, took her away just in time. Acting as the dog's foster mother, Nan was driving Lulu to her new home in nearby Decatur in 2002.

While the car was zipping through traffic on I-285, Lulu stuck her head out the open window and let the wind blow in her face. Then, for some strange reason, she leaped out.

Nan screamed as she saw Lulu bounce up in the air and

then roll and roll while cars were swerving all over to avoid her. When Lulu quit rolling, she scrambled to her feet and started running straight up the center lane of the interstate. At least six people stopped their cars to see if they could help Lulu. Finally, Nan was able to catch her. Amazingly, Lulu suffered only cuts and bruises but no serious injuries.

"If anyone deserves a great home, it's this little dog," said Nan. After suffering a rough life, then facing death row and surviving a seventy-mile-an-hour leap onto a busy highway, "she just needs a nice, safe place — with rolled-up windows."

See Ya Later, Alligator

There's an old saying that goes: "It's not the size of the dog in the fight that matters, it's the size of the fight in the dog."

Blue, a two-year-old Australian blue heeler, proved the truth of that saying when he fought a huge twelve-foot alligator to save the life of his eighty-five-year-old mistress.

One evening in 2001, Ruth Gay of LaBelle, Florida, was walking with her dog along a canal behind her house. Ruth fell face-first, breaking her nose and dislocating her shoulder. Unable to get up, she yelled for help, but no one was nearby to hear her. Meanwhile, Blue lay by her side, giving her comfort as she petted him.

Suddenly, Blue growled and ran off into the darkness. Seconds later, Ruth heard hissing, snapping, and barking. The injured woman knew instantly that Blue was trying to protect her from a large alligator that had climbed out of the water and was heading right toward her. Ruth's heart sank because she figured that a fifty-pound dog was no match for a full-grown gator ten times his size.

Barking and growling, Blue fought off the reptile just twenty yards away from Ruth. She winced every time she heard her valiant dog yelp because she knew it meant he had been bitten. But Blue refused to let the gator get any closer to the helpless woman, even if it meant risking his life.

After several tense minutes, the fighting stopped and Blue returned to Ruth's side, where he stood guard, waiting for the gator to return. A short while later, it came back, so the dog took off to battle it once again. Hearing Blue yelp and whine, Ruth knew he was getting hurt. Then the fighting stopped and Blue didn't return. Ruth thought he was dead.

But Blue wasn't dead. He was, however, badly hurt

from more than two dozen bite wounds. Having driven off the gator for the second time, Ruth's faithful dog lay in the grass, bleeding. When relatives showed up at the house more than an hour after the first attack, Blue found the strength to run to their car and bark and jump. Understanding that he was trying to tell them something, they followed Blue, who led them to his injured mistress.

The elderly woman was rushed to the hospital, where she remained for six weeks, recovering from shoulder surgery. She made a complete recovery.

Meanwhile, Blue was taken to Suburban Animal Hospital, where veterinarian Dr. Terry Terlep successfully treated the dog. Like his owner, Blue made a full recovery. "It's amazing what an animal will do in a time of need," Dr. Terlep said. "He's a pretty brave dog."

Blaze of Glory

When Budweiser the Saint Bernard was ten months old, his owner was fed up with him and tried to give him away because he didn't get along with the dog. The owner couldn't get any takers until Mr. and Mrs. B. M. Carter of John's Island, South Carolina, came along. After the Carters looked the dog in the eye, they believed he wasn't the nasty dog that his owner claimed he was, so they adopted him.

They were glad they did. So were their six grandchildren, who loved playing with the gentle, sweet dog whenever they came to visit. Budweiser enjoyed them, too, letting them hug him and ride on his back.

In 1972, several months after the dog had been adopted, the grandkids came over to spend the night at the Carter home. Grandpa was working in his restaurant when, back home, Grandma was putting the kids to bed. Suddenly, the house was rocked by two explosions and burst into flames. Everyone froze in terror.

That's when the 165-pound Saint Bernard sprang into action. Budweiser bounded from the porch and into the house. He immediately went into the nearest bedroom where the youngest child, four-year-old Linda Lawson, was in the corner, crying. Biting down on her T-shirt, Budweiser dragged her safely out of the burning house.

Then he dashed back into the smoke and fire and found five-year-old Joyce Hinson. He gently took her arm in his mouth and led her out the door.

Meanwhile, Grandma Carter rounded up the four other children and ushered them to safety. Thirty minutes later, the roof collapsed and the entire house was destroyed. Fire officials later discovered that a faulty gas pipe had triggered the explosions.

Fortunately, no one in the family was injured — except Budweiser. The brave, heroic Saint Bernard suffered burned paws and smoke inhalation (breathing in too much smoke). But the dog, who at one time nobody wanted, recovered quickly, thanks to all the love he received from his grateful family.

Strike Three, You're Out

Mariah, a ninety-pound rottweiler, grabbed a baseball bat and saved her master from an attack by three would-be robbers.

Ever since she was eight months old, Mariah had been riding in the cab of the truck of her master, long-distance driver Herb Blish of Andover, New Hampshire. She had traveled across the country with him, keeping him company while he was on the road. The highway dog even had her own bunk bed in the cab.

One day in 1995, the seventeen-month-old dog was sleeping in the cab when they pulled into a truck stop near Walcott, Iowa. Herb had planned to bring back her favorite treat, beef jerky. As he stepped out into the parking lot, Herb faced two young men who demanded money from him. He refused, not knowing that a third man, who was holding a baseball bat, was hiding behind the truck.

All of a sudden, Herb heard a yelp and a growl and a man's voice yell, "He's got a rottweiler!" It was the man with the bat. When he saw Mariah snarling and flashing her piercing eyes, he dropped the bat and ran off.

Mariah limped from behind the truck, her hair standing on end. In her mouth, she was holding the fat end of the baseball bat. When the other two attackers saw the fierce dog carrying the bat and baring her teeth, they fled.

Mariah had scared them off even though she was injured. When she had seen her master threatened, she had leaped seven feet out the window of the cab. She had landed so hard that she had torn some ligaments in her right hind leg. But the pain from her injury hadn't stopped her from grabbing the bat away from one of the attackers.

Mariah needed to wear a cast on her injured leg and stay home for three weeks. When Herb went on the road without her during her recovery, Mariah whined. Said Herb, "She doesn't even like me moving my truck in the driveway unless she's in it."

Titanic Dog

A pet dog was hailed as a hero in the greatest sea disaster of all time — the sinking of the *Titanic*.

Rigel was a black Newfoundland owned by William McMaster Murdoch, who was the first officer of the luxury ocean liner on its first and only voyage from England to America. On the night of April 14, 1912, in the north Atlantic, the *Titanic* struck an iceberg and sank, taking 1,595 passengers and crew members to a watery grave.

Rigel survived along with 745 people who found safety in lifeboats. But, according to news reports, survivors in one lifeboat owed their lives to the dog.

After the *Titanic* sank, the Newfoundland spent more than three hours in frigid water, desperately searching for his master. Meanwhile, the steamship *Carpathia* was the first vessel to arrive at the scene and search for survivors.

The *Carpathia* was moving slowly in the dark, looking

for boats, rafts, or anything floating that could hold a survivor. The steamship's captain, Arthur Rostron, wasn't aware that a lifeboat was drifting right below the big vessel's starboard (right side) bow. Although they were in danger of being rammed, the terror-stricken men and women in the lifeboat were too weak to shout a warning loud enough to reach the captain.

Here's what happened next, according to the *New York Herald*: "The boat might not have been seen were it not for the sharp barking of Rigel, who was swimming ahead of the craft and valiantly announcing his position. The barks attracted the attention of Captain Rostron and he went to the starboard end . . . and saw the boat. He immediately ordered the engines stopped and the lifeboat came alongside the starboard gangway.

"Care was taken to take Rigel aboard, but he appeared little affected by his long trip through the ice-cold water."

The dog was praised for his courage and smarts in saving the lives of those in the lifeboat. But Rigel never had a chance to save the life of the one person who was the most important to him. His owner had gone down with the ship.

A Gift From Carly

Carly Simon had been an unwanted dog who had known little love in the first year of her life. But when Kathie Webber and her husband, Chuck, adopted the chocolate Labrador retriever, they turned her into a happy, loving pet. The dog — named after the famous pop singer — soon repaid that love in a big way.

Right before Christmas 2001, there was an unusual cold snap in Ocala, Florida, and Kathie was busy covering her plants from frost while Carly watched. Kathie wasn't used to below-freezing temperatures, so she had bundled up with extra pairs of socks, jeans, sweaters, and coats. She could hardly move from wearing all the bulky clothes.

Suddenly, while covering her orange tree next to the pool, Kathie slipped and plunged into the deep end. Down she sank, ten feet under. By the time her feet hit the bottom, all the layers of clothing were soaked and now weighed about one hundred pounds. She couldn't move or scream. There was nothing she could do.

I'm drowning, she thought in a panic. *I can't believe I'm going to drown here in my swimming pool.*

Just then, she heard a terrible howl and big splash. It was Carly diving into the pool. The dog circled around Kathie's head for a few seconds. Then Carly stopped and dipped her hindquarters down so Kathie could grip her tail.

Kathie grabbed hold and Carly started to swim with all her might, towing Kathie and her soaked clothing. The dog was pulling about two hundred pounds, but she never stopped paddling. Slowly but surely, she dragged Kathie to the shallow end of the pool until her mistress could stick her head above the water. When Carly was sure Kathie was safe, she covered her face with kisses.

"It was the best Christmas present I ever received," Kathie said. Since then the once unwanted, unhappy dog has been spoiled and pampered and treated like a queen. And why not? She deserves it.

A Bite out of Crime

A pet dog not only chased down a burglar and held him at bay until police arrived, but the canine appeared in court and helped convict him, too.

Screenwriter Jack Barton Loeb was working on a script in his New York apartment late at night in 1937 when he heard his wire-haired terrier, Rusty Bud, barking in the other room. When Loeb went to investigate, he found his dog chasing a burglar around the living room. Loeb lunged after the man while Rusty Bud kept nipping at the thief's ankles.

But the burglar managed to break free from Loeb's grasp and dashed out of the apartment, down the stairs, and out the door — with Rusty Bud in hot pursuit. After calling the police, Loeb, who was still in his pajamas, went looking for his dog. Minutes later, he found him. Rusty Bud had cornered the burglar in front of a nearby apartment. Growling and snarling, the five-year-old terrier threatened to bite the thief if he dared make the slightest move.

"Call him off! Call him off!" the trembling burglar pleaded to Loeb. "He's been biting my ankles!" Only after police arrived did Loeb tell his valiant dog to relax. But that wasn't the last time the robber, Frank Lucca, would see the dog.

Police charged Lucca, a thief who sported a long criminal record, with attempted burglary. Six weeks later, at his trial, Lucca claimed he was innocent. But he changed his tune when Loeb brought Rusty Bud into court.

The dog was placed on the prosecutor's table in front of the jury box and immediately recognized Lucca. The terrier growled at him as his master testified against the robber. Knowing he was beat, Lucca told the judge that he wanted to change his plea to guilty.

As the criminal was led out of the courtroom, Rusty Bud lunged after him and tried to nip at his ankles. "Don't let him get me!" Lucca howled as he ducked behind a guard.

Said Judge Owen Bohan, "There's something about that dog which lets you know he means business."

Jet Power

Candy Sangster had a special bond with her pet Doberman pinscher, Jet. The dog seemed to know when her mistress wasn't feeling well and would lick her hand to cheer her up. That special bond saved Candy's life.

On Halloween 1987, Candy was preparing for trick-or-treaters who soon would be calling at her house in Sepulveda, California. Her husband, George, was out of town and no one was home with her except her six-year-old dog. Suddenly, Candy began to feel faint. Jet trotted into the living room just as Candy, a diabetic, began weaving back and forth before falling unconscious onto the floor.

Knowing that her mistress was in serious trouble, Jet nuzzled open the front door, which Candy had left ajar for the trick-or-treaters. Then the dog dashed outside and ran to the gate of a four-foot-tall fence that separated the Sangsters' property from their next-door neighbor Helen

Lavin. Although the gate was latched, Jet cleverly managed to push up the latch with her paws and nuzzle it open.

The dog sprinted to Helen's house and barked furiously. When Helen opened the door, she knew something was wrong because Jet was normally a quiet, well-behaved dog. Helen noticed that Candy's car was in the driveway and the lights were on at her house, so she called Candy. When there was no answer, Helen dialed 911 and explained the situation.

Meanwhile, Jet kept barking and running back and forth between the two houses. When the police arrived at Helen's house, she pointed to Jet and said, "She's telling us something. I think we should go over to the Sangsters'."

They found Candy lying unconscious on the floor. When Helen explained that Candy was a diabetic, paramedics were summoned and quickly determined that she was suffering from severe hypoglycemia, a lack of sugar in her blood. They gave her glucose, a kind of sugar, and she soon regained consciousness.

"The paramedics told me that if it hadn't been for Jet, I wouldn't have survived," Candy said later. "A friend had given me Jet when she was just eight weeks old. She's the best gift I've ever received."

Patches to the Rescue

When Marvin Scott and his wife moved to their lake-front home in Spanaway, Washington, they brought with them their Labrador retriever and a basset hound. They soon had a third dog — Patches, a collie-malamute who belonged to a neighbor. Patches played with the Scotts' dogs, shared their food, and spent most of his time at the Scotts' house. So Marvin asked the neighbor if he could buy Patches, which he did for twenty-five dollars.

It was the best purchase Marvin ever made.

About two years later, on a bitter, windy December night in 1964, Marvin decided to check on the condition of a boat that was moored to a pier behind his house. With the temperatures plunging near zero, he was afraid that the boat would be damaged by ice. So he bundled up and, with Patches tagging along, trudged to the pier. Marvin noticed that ice was building up on the boat and that the spray from the lake waves had frozen on the pier, making it extremely slippery.

Caught by a strong gust of wind, the sixty-four-year-old man lost his balance on the slick pier and fell off. He slammed into a floating dock below, ripping muscles and tendons in his leg. The seriously injured man then rolled off the dock and plunged into the frigid fifteen-foot-deep water and began sinking.

Seeing what had happened to his master, the eighty-five-pound dog immediately leaped into the lake. Then, with his teeth, he grabbed the two-hundred-pound man by the hair and towed him to the floating dock. Patches jumped out of the water and expected Marvin to get out, too. But because he was badly hurt and awfully cold, Marvin couldn't move his legs and fell back into the deadly water.

So Patches dived into the lake again. Once more, the dog towed his master to the floating dock and climbed out. Understanding that Marvin couldn't get out of the water on his own, Patches braced his paws on the dock, grabbed the man's collar by his teeth, and tugged. Marvin gathered all the strength he could muster and slowly pulled himself onto the floating dock.

With great effort, he climbed onto the pier and then, with Patches yanking on his collar, Marvin began crawling up a rocky three-hundred-foot slope toward his home. When he was about twenty feet from the house, he was too exhausted to go any farther. So Patches began barking while Marvin threw a rock against the door until his wife came outside.

Marvin was rushed to the hospital, where he remained in critical condition for twenty-five days. It took him more than six months to recover.

Said Marvin later, "If it hadn't been for Patches, I'd be dead."

Thirst for Life

When sixty-three-year-old farmer Herbert Jones lay paralyzed for days on the ground with a broken back, he thought he would die there because no one was around. But he hadn't counted on his faithful canine companion, Cocoa, to keep him alive.

Jones tended a pecan grove that he owned near Umatilla, Florida. He lived alone except for his two pets, Cocoa, a small brown mutt, and a black snake.

In 1953, Jones was pruning a tree in the middle of his grove when he fell off his ladder and broke his back. Paralyzed from the fall, he couldn't move and his shouts weren't heard by anyone except Cocoa. The dog ran to his side and stayed with the seriously injured man.

Jones ordered Cocoa to go get help, but for two days the dog refused to leave his master. By now, the farmer was dying of thirst. "Water, Cocoa, water," Jones mumbled over and over. "Please, get me some water."

Finally, Cocoa understood and went over to the water pail near the house. For the next three days, the dog ran back and forth between the water pail and his master. Cocoa would drink from the pail and then return to Jones and let drops of water from the dog's tongue drip into the man's parched throat.

Cocoa also brought Jones his pet black snake, which the farmer had taught the dog to play with. The snake rested on Jones's stomach and kept him company.

Five agonizing days after the accident, a friend arrived at the house. Cocoa ran up to him and kept barking until he followed the dog to the fallen farmer. Jones was then taken to the hospital and eventually recovered.

Said Jones, "That dog saved my life."

Unlikely Hero

The owner of an unwanted, deaf Dalmatian with a crooked jaw had been advised to put the dog to sleep. But she refused. Because of that decision, a little girl was saved from certain death.

Sophie was one of ten newborn Dalmatian pups in a litter belonging to breeder Robbie McHenry of Corsock Mill, Scotland. But Sophie had serious birth defects. She was deaf, had one blue and one brown eye, and her jaw was so twisted that she couldn't eat anything hard unless it was broken up for her.

Other breeders told Robbie to put the dog down, but by that time Sophie was seven weeks old and had developed her own character. Robbie just couldn't do it.

Unfortunately, no one wanted the dog. While searching for a permanent home for Sophie, Robbie temporarily left the dog with the Peck family in 2002. The very next day, the six-month-old Dalmatian puppy who nobody wanted became a hero.

Five-year-old Georgia Peck had wandered down to the Urr River near Galloway, Scotland, after the dog had trotted down to the bank. Suddenly, Georgia lost her footing and fell into the swift-moving water. She cried out for help as she was swept downstream. Although Sophie couldn't hear Georgia's desperate screams, she saw the little girl was drowning and plunged into the water. Fighting the current, the puppy swam over to the thrashing youngster and let her grab one of Sophie's hind legs. Then the Dalmatian dragged Georgia back to safety.

"As soon as I fell in, Sophie came over and got me," Georgia said once she recovered from her ordeal. "I held on to her paw, and she swam with me to the side. I couldn't have got out of the water without Sophie's paw. She saved me. She couldn't hear me screaming but still she saved me."

Homeward Bound

Back in 1855 in Portsmouth, New Hampshire, a cruel person who hated dogs left poisoned meat in the streets at night. The owner of Bruno, a highly prized pointer, feared that his dog might also become a victim, so he decided to send him away from the danger. He gave Bruno to Herman Eldredge, the captain of a freighter, who took the dog to Manhattan aboard his ship.

The captain then sold Bruno to a gentleman who admired the pointer's remarkable beauty and intelligence. The new owner took the dog on the ferry from Manhattan to Staten Island where he lived and tied him in his yard, which was enclosed by a seven-foot fence. The man fed the dog and petted him in an effort to make him happy in his new home.

The owner was surprised the next morning when he found that Bruno had gnawed off his rope, cleared the fence, and escaped. The man took the ferry from Staten Island to Manhattan and went immediately to the wharf to complain to Captain Eldredge. But the ship had already sailed for Portsmouth.

The man then went into the shipping office and learned that Bruno had been seen earlier walking around the wharf, shortly after the ship had left. Thinking he had lost his dog for good, the man returned to his home on Staten Island. He was astonished at what he saw. There in the yard was Bruno, happily gnawing on a bone!

The stunned owner sat down with the dog and figured out what had happened.

After cleverly escaping the fenced yard of his new master, Bruno made his way to the Staten Island ferry and took it to Manhattan. Then he walked the city's unfamiliar streets to find — out of dozens of wharves — the one where Captain Eldredge's ship was docked. He wanted to take the ship back to his original home in Portsmouth.

Unfortunately, the ship had left shortly before Bruno had arrived at the wharf. Incredibly, the dog had then retraced his steps and taken the ferry back to Staten Island, where he returned to his new home. Talk about a smart dog!

Up and Running

Like most border collies, Meg does a fine job of herding sheep. Unlike any other border collie, she carries out her work on just two legs.

She simply refused to give up despite being the victim of two serious accidents. In 2001, when Meg was three years old, her front left leg was amputated after she was hit by a car. She quickly recovered and went back to work on three legs. But six months later, she was struck by a four-wheel all-terrain vehicle, which crushed her right rear leg and it had to be amputated.

Meg, who works on a two-hundred-acre farm in Maungati, New Zealand, may not be as quick as she was with all four legs but she still does an admirable job, according to her owner, Ian McDonald.

Responding to Ian's instructions and whistles as he puts her through her paces, Meg moves with ease around a small flock of sheep. The only difference from a four-legged dog is that she drops down the moment she stops running.

"She's a dear dog," said Ian. "She is strong-eyed and does the job."

He admitted that many other farmers wouldn't have kept a dog with two legs, but there was something about Meg's personality that made him spend several thousand dollars for her operations.

"She's quite an amazing dog," said local veterinarian Marnie Crilly. "She's very healthy and out rounding up the sheep."

As if it wasn't strange enough to have a two-legged dog, Ian also has another working dog, Sam, who is sixteen and deaf.

Scooby Knew What to Do

After running away and getting hit by a car, Scooby the shih tzu knew exactly what to do. He limped right to the nearest animal clinic and checked himself in.

The six-year-old dog had been tied up in the backyard of his owner, Shirley Farris of Corbin, Kentucky. But when a thunderstorm blew in one morning in 2003, Scooby was scared and broke the collar ring of his harness and ran off before Shirley could bring him inside. Unbeknownst to Shirley, the dog scampered across the street and was struck by a vehicle, injuring his leg and tail. Although he was hurt, the dog limped away before anyone could help him.

While Shirley went looking for him, Scooby somehow hobbled several blocks to the Corbin Animal Clinic and was waiting on the doorstep when employees arrived for work. The dog followed them inside and limped straight into the operating room. Although Scooby had been there before, he didn't have his tags on, so the staff wasn't sure who he was. Nevertheless, he was treated for his injuries.

Meanwhile, Shirley was very upset. She kept calling the police department and neighbors and dog pounds, looking for Scooby. Then she thought, *There's one chance out of a million that someone might have taken him to the animal clinic.* So she called the vet. To her great joy, Scooby was there.

"Who was the nice person who brought him in?" she asked a staff member.

"No one," replied the staffer. "He came in on his own."

Scooby obviously knew the animal clinic was the place to get help. There were subdivisions with hundreds of houses between his home and the vet's office, yet he knew where to go.

Like everyone else, Scooby's veterinarian, Dr. Gerald Majors, was amazed that the injured dog could find his way to the animal clinic. "We'd like to think that he was smart enough to come here for help. He'd been here a few times. He knew this was the right place."

Trial by Fire

When fire broke out in a boardinghouse, nothing mattered to Topsy the Boston terrier except saving her two puppies. Even though both her rear legs were paralyzed and she was trapped by flames, she was determined to find a way for the three of them to survive.

Topsy, who lived in a boardinghouse in New York City, had lost the use of her hind legs after giving birth to her pups in 1905. Despite her disability, she still nursed them and cared for them, and showed everyone she was a good mother.

But not until the blaze did everyone realize just how brave and dedicated a mother she really was.

When fire broke out, Topsy carried one of her three-week-old pups between her teeth and tried to crawl out of the room. But because of her paralysis, it took her a long time. When she finally reached the only exit, it was cut off by the flames. However, there was a doorway to another room that wasn't on fire yet, so she crawled into it and left the puppy there. Then she went back and got the other pup and brought it into the room.

But her troubles were far from over. It had taken her so long to move her puppies that by now the fire had spread into this room as well. Topsy, however, wasn't ready to give up. Even though she was disabled, she crawled up on a sofa and tried to dig a hole in the mattress, believing the puppies would be safe there. Being a dog, she couldn't have known that the sofa would burn up quicker than anything else in the room once the flames reached it.

But the firemen reached the sofa before the fire did. The room was thick with smoke when they turned on the hose and beat back the flames. Suddenly, one of the firemen shouted, "Men, will you look at that?"

The firemen crowded around, and there was Topsy still digging for dear life into the sofa. One of the puppies was already inside the sofa, while the mother was working hard to make room for the other. "It's obvious that the dog never thought of herself," said the fireman, "because she could never have made the hole big enough for three."

The firemen brought Topsy and her pups safely out of the burning building. They were not harmed.

When Topsy's owner, Moses Johnson, learned of her rescue attempts, he said, "It just shows how strong a mother's love can be."

No Place Like Home

Tigger was a half-blind, deaf, thirteen-year-old shih tzu who was so old and feeble that her owners were thinking about putting her to sleep. Well, she showed them she still had plenty of life left in her.

The miniature dog was spending the weekend with dog-sitters while her owners, Bonnie and Dennis Lila of Plover, Wisconsin, hosted a wedding shower at their home across town in 2001. Early Sunday morning, Tigger was let outside. With her disabilities, she had never wandered very far from her house. But Tigger knew she wasn't at her house; she was at someone else's — and she wanted to be home. So she headed off.

Moments later, when her sitters looked outside, they were upset that she had vanished. After searching the neighborhood for several hours without success, they worried that something bad had happened to the little dog. They decided to drive over to Bonnie and Dennis's home and break the bad news to them.

When the sitters arrived, they were stunned. There in the house was none other than Tigger! Amazingly, despite her poor eyesight and lack of hearing, the shih tzu had trotted through yards, on sidewalks, and across busy streets to make it back home. She had walked clear across town for four miles, and she did it in less than six hours.

"For her, that was quite an accomplishment," Bonnie Lila told the *Green Bay Press-Gazette*. She said that a week before Tigger's big adventure, the family talked about having her put down because she was sick, but they didn't have the heart to do it. Tigger then proved she was a lot stronger than her family thought. "The older she gets, the more stubborn she gets," said Bonnie.

Super Fly

When a runaway horse wildly pulled a sleigh through the snowy streets of South Orange, New Jersey, a fox terrier named Fly flew to the rescue.

The dog often rode with his owner, Christopher Munther, who drove a horse-drawn sleigh. Fly got along fine with the horse and sometimes, to the amusement of onlookers, would ride on the horse's back as it pulled the sleigh.

One time in 1904, Fly was sitting in the sleigh when something spooked the horse and it took off without Munther. Men, women, and children scattered as the horse and the sleigh zigzagged down the street. In a remarkable display of canine smarts, Fly tried to stop the horse by tugging on the reins with his teeth just as he had seen his owner do many times.

Unfortunately, the frightened horse refused to stop, so

Fly jumped off the sleigh and dashed in front of the horse. Then he started barking at it, trying to slow it down. When that failed, the dog hopped back into the sleigh and once again pulled on the reins. This time, the horse slowed down just enough for two bystanders to grab its bridle.

But as they started to lead it away, Fly jumped off the sleigh, growling and snarling at the men to back away from the horse, which they did. Then Fly stood guard until his owner arrived.

Amazingly, that wasn't the first time Fly had stopped the horse from running away. Just days earlier, the horse had taken off without the driver. Fly raced after the sleigh, jumped aboard, and yanked on the reins until the horse slowed to a trot. Said his owner, "Fly is a clever animal."

America's Greatest War Dog

A small, stray bull terrier who an American soldier smuggled aboard a troop ship to France ended up becoming the most decorated dog of World War I.

Stubby — named after his short tail — was the pet of Private John Conroy, who hid the dog from his commanding officer until they reached the battlefield in 1917. When the commander found out about the dog, Conroy talked him into making Stubby the mascot of the 102nd Infantry.

The war was fought from trenches where life was often cold, wet, and very dangerous. Stubby had to work overtime to keep up his troops' morale. Soon after his arrival, the German enemy launched a gas attack on the American soldiers. The gas was extremely deadly, burning their skin and eyes and blistering their lungs. Stubby was hurt by the gas but recovered in a field hospital.

He was now supersensitive to even the smallest amount of gas. When the Germans quietly launched another gas attack while the Americans were sleeping, Stubby immediately sensed its deadly presence. He began barking loudly and running through the trench, tugging at their uniforms and boots to wake them up. Because of the dog's quick action, the men put on their gas masks and were saved from serious injury.

During battles, Stubby looked for wounded soldiers in the zone between the German and American trenches, known as no-man's-land. As bullets whizzed by him, he would find injured men and bark out their location so medics could rescue them.

One day in no-man's-land, Stubby found a German spy who then tried to run away. The dog chased him and bit his legs until he fell. Then Stubby chomped on the spy's rear end, holding him down until American soldiers captured him.

Stubby served in seventeen battles and survived near death after a grenade exploded not far from him during one attack. After the war ended in 1918, Stubby returned to the United States, where he marched in parades and was given dozens of medals. He met famous people, including Presidents Woodrow Wilson, Warren Harding, and Calvin Coolidge. Whenever he met important people, Stubby would give them his doggy salute. He would sit up and put his right paw over his right eye. And many people would return the salute to America's greatest war dog.

Keeping Faith

A mongrel named Faith was born without either of her front legs, yet she plays and chases cats like most any other dog. How? She walks upright just like a human.

It's not unusual to see dogs stand up to greet their loved ones, or even to rise up to beg for a treat, but Faith remains upright and actually gets around that way.

In January 2003, Reuben Stringfellow, seventeen, of Oklahoma City, Oklahoma, brought home the deformed puppy. It had come from a litter of his friend's dog, who had rejected the pup. Dogs with birth defects are rarely rescued and given a chance, but the Stringfellow family fell in love with the three-week-old puppy. The Stringfellows were willing to put in the time, money, and effort to care for her because they had faith in her. So that's what they named her.

"Even though Faith has this defect, we taught her to

stand, hop, and eventually walk on her two back legs, like a human," said Reuben's mother, Laura, a schoolteacher. "She's been a great dog and we forget she's handicapped. You'll turn around and she's chasing the geese at the park, running, jumping, skipping, and acting like any other dog . . . well, any other dog with a nose reach of forty inches from the ground."

Faith has become quite a celebrity, appearing on national TV talk shows and in newspapers and magazines throughout the world. She even has her own Web site, *http://www.geocities.com/jude_stringfellow/index.htm*.

"I take Faith to school and to class with me," said Laura. "She is an inspiration to every student who feels that they just can't get up in the morning or do their homework. She is truly a miracle worker."

Diamond in the Ruff

A golden retriever puppy who had been tied to a lamp-post and abandoned was brought to the dog pound in Mount Holly, New Jersey, in 1999.

When Renee Herskowitz — a volunteer who tries to find homes for unwanted retrievers — first saw this pup, she didn't have much hope. He was filthy with fur like dirty straw and he acted like a wild animal. Worst of all, the pound's veterinarian said the puppy had a weak heart and would probably die in a year or two.

Officials at the pound figured no one would ever adopt such a scraggly, unruly, sick puppy and planned to put him to sleep. That's when Renee decided that if no one else was going to give the dog a chance at life, she would. Renee adopted the pup and named him Breeze.

No one knew that the dog had an amazing, rare talent.

But Renee had a special feeling about Breeze. One reason was that they had something in common. Like the puppy, Renee had received bad medical news. Her doctors found that she had a disease that weakens the body's nervous system and causes seizures (severe twitches and fainting). There is no cure, although there are treatments to keep it under control. Everyone thought that because she was sick, Renee couldn't care for a difficult dog. But deep down Renee knew that she had to try.

She took Breeze to a veterinarian who specializes in heart problems in dogs. The vet gave her medicine for the dog's heart condition. Then she started training Breeze. He was an excellent student and learned his lessons well. With good care, his coat turned to golden silk and his behavior improved. They became best friends.

About a month after adopting Breeze, Renee was in her sunroom when Breeze flew through the door and kept barking loudly at her as if saying, "Come with me!" Renee gently tried to brush him off. Instead, he grabbed her pant leg and started pulling her toward the door, then up the stairs and into her bedroom, where he pushed her down onto her bed.

Seconds later, Renee suffered a seizure. Had she stayed downstairs, she might have fallen. Somehow Breeze knew that she was about to faint and that he had to get her up to her soft bed so she wouldn't get hurt.

At first no one believed Renee's story about Breeze. Dogs can't tell when a person is going to become sick, they said. But that's not true.

Scientists believe that a few special dogs have a talent for predicting when a person is going to become sick. No one knows how. It is a skill that can't be taught. Dogs who are born with this gift are very rare and very precious. They're the diamonds of the dog world. Breeze, the dirty wild puppy who no one wanted, is one of these diamonds.

After that day, Renee continued to have seizures. Each time Breeze would warn her before they happened. Sometimes he would not let her leave the house because he knew a seizure was minutes away.

Today, Breeze is an officially recognized, trained service dog who wears a vest to carry her medicines. Now he can go everywhere with Renee — to work and stores as well as on planes and trains. He's always by her side, ready to warn her of a seizure or to break her fall if she faints.

Renee saved Breeze's life and now he is saving hers. "He's my guardian angel," she says.